Inspiring Stories for Amazing Girls

Who Believe in Themselves

21 Short Stories About Courage, Self-Confidence, Overcoming Fear & Empowering Young Minds in Just 5 Minutes a Day

By
Sati Siroda

Book Ecke

Inspiring Stories for Amazing Girls Who Believe in Themselves

21 Short Stories About Courage, Self-Confidence, Overcoming Fear & Empowering Young Minds in Just 5 Minutes a Day

By

Sati Siroda

Published by Book Ecke
154, 4th Floor, City Vista, Tower A,
Suite No.1140, Fountain Road, Kharadi, Pune - 411014
Website: www.bookecke.com

© Copyright Sati Siroda, 2025 - All rights reserved.

The content contained within this book may not be reproduced, duplicated or transmitted without direct written permission from the author or the publisher.

Under no circumstances will any blame or legal responsibility be held against the publisher or author for any damages, reparation, or monetary loss due to the information contained within this book. Either directly or indirectly. You are responsible for your own choices, actions, and results.

Legal Notice:

This book is copyright-protected. This book is only for personal use. You cannot amend, distribute, sell, use, quote or paraphrase any part or the content within this book without the consent of the author or publisher.

Disclaimer Notice:

Please note the information contained within this document is for educational and entertainment purposes only. All effort has been executed to present accurate, up-to-date, and reliable, complete information. No warranties of any kind are declared or implied. Readers acknowledge that the author is not engaging in the rendering of legal, financial, medical or professional advice. The content within this book has been derived from various sources. Please consult a licensed professional before attempting any techniques outlined in this book. Fair use of AI tools has been employed selectively to enhance the creation of this book.

By reading this document, the reader agrees that under no circumstances is the author responsible for any losses, direct or indirect, which are incurred as a result of the use of the information contained within this document, including, but not limited to, — errors, omissions, or inaccuracies. For permission requests, contact **support@bookecke.com**.

ISBN
eBook: 978-81-966458-8-5
Paperback: 978-81-985337-3-9
Hardback: 978-81-985337-5-3

First edition [2025]

Visit www.bookecke.com for any further information.

To every amazing girl who dares to dream, to every brave soul who takes that first step, and to every heart that believes in its own magic—this book is for you. May you always find the courage to shine and the confidence to chase your brightest dreams.

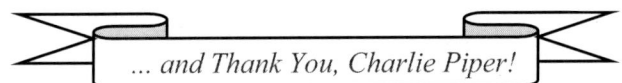
... and Thank You, Charlie Piper!

BOOKS BY SATI SIRODA

Mind the Quote

Coffee Tales: Short Stories of Wisdom

Earnest Poetica: Ink Expressions of the Ineffable Heart

Gratitude Journal: Reflect, Appreciate, Transform in 60 Days

Table of Contents

Introduction vii

Part 1: The Courage to Begin..1

    Chapter 1: Emma's Secret Garden 2

    Chapter 2: Jamie and the Great Science Fair Challenge..............................6

    Chapter 3: Ellie's Big Day at the Treehouse..10

Part 2: The Confidence Code 14

    Chapter 4: Lily and the Secret Choir Audition 15

    Chapter 5: Maine and the Great Rock-Climbing Adventure........................19

Part 3: Facing Your Fears 23

    Chapter 6: Shanaya and the Mystery of the Forest Trail 24

    Chapter 7: Zara and the Great Math Exam Adventure 28

    Chapter 8: Maria and the Power of Self-Talk 32

Part 4: Resilience: Bouncing Back Stronger 36

    Chapter 9: Laura and the Big Swim Challenge 37

    Chapter 10: The Secret to Tina's Triumph 41

    Chapter 11: Eliza and the Garden of Perseverance...................................45

Part 5: Compassion and Connection 49

    Chapter 12: Ava and the Kindness Challenge 50

    Chapter 13: Dahlia and the Friendship Circle 54

Part 6: Dream Big, Act Boldly 58

    Chapter 14: Maggie and the Power of Big Dreams....................................59

    Chapter 15: Aurora and the Black Belt Quest 63

    Chapter 16: Victoria and the Bold School Club..67

Part 7: The Role of Gratitude 71

Chapter 17: Isabella and the Gratitude Adventure 72

Chapter 18: Nora and the Power of Gratitude 76

Part 8: Celebrating Your Inner Superstar *80*

Chapter 19: Violet and the Puppy Rescue Mission 81

Chapter 20: Hazel and the Courage to Shine 85

Chapter 21: Eleanor and the Call of the Music 89

The Journey Ahead *93*

Your Free Gift

Hi there, Rockstar! ✺

I have a special surprise just for you—not one, but **TWO** incredible e-books to make your day even brighter! These free gifts are packed with fun, creativity, and inspiration:

1. **Penguin Coloring Book with Fun Facts**
Get ready for:
   - Gorgeous animal illustrations to bring to life with your favorite colors.
   - Fascinating fun facts about penguins to learn as you color!

2. **Unstoppable You: 10 Inspiring Stories for Young Achievers**
Jump into:

   - 10 best tales that inspire imagination and curiosity.

   - Adventures with lessons and empowering affirmations!

Just ask your awesome grown-up to scan the QR code to grab your free e-books!

Scan Me

Introduction

Heya, Amazing Girl!

What's up?

First off, let me tell you a little secret: YOU are absolutely incredible. Yep, you read that right! Inside you, there's a world of courage, creativity, and kindness just waiting to shine. And guess what? This book is here to help you discover all that awesomeness.

Welcome to *Inspiring Stories for Amazing Girls Who Believe In Themselves*! This book is like your very own treasure chest, filled with fun and inspiring stories. The best part? You can unlock these treasures in just 5 minutes a day—how cool is that?

What This Book Is All About

Have you ever felt a little scared to try something new? Or maybe you've worried about messing up? Don't worry—everyone feels that way sometimes (even grown-ups!). But here's the thing: those little worries can actually be stepping stones to something amazing. With the stories in this book, you'll learn how to turn your fears into fuel and your doubts into confidence.

Each story is packed with adventures, lessons, and characters who face challenges just like you do. Whether it's standing up for a friend, trying out for a team, or just believing in your own ideas, these stories will show you how to be the heroine of your own life.

Why You'll Love It

Here's what makes this book super special:

- The stories are short and easy to read—perfect for a quick break.

- Every story has a little secret: a lesson to help you grow braver and stronger.
- At the end of each story, there is an affirmation to make you stronger and activities for you to try.
- And most importantly, it's all about YOU becoming your most fantastic self!

Why I Wrote This Book (Just for You!)

When I was your age, I also felt shy and unsure of myself. But then I discovered that stories have the magical power to make you feel brave and unstoppable. That's why I wanted to share these stories with you—so you can feel that magic, too. You are capable of so much more than you know, and this book is here to help you see that.

Ready to Begin?

Okay, amazing girl, let's get started! Grab a cozy spot, maybe a snack, and dive into the first story. Are you ready to see just how incredible you really are?

Let's go—your adventure starts NOW!

With love,

Sati

Part 1: The Courage to Begin

Hi again, Superstar!

Do you know what the hardest part of any journey is? Yep, you guessed it—taking that very first step. It can feel scary, right? But here's a little secret: every big dream, every amazing adventure, and every success story you've ever heard about started with someone being brave enough to begin.

So, are you ready to take that first step? Let's go—your journey is just getting started!

Chapter 1: Emma's Secret Garden

Emma stood at the edge of her backyard, staring at the overgrown bushes near the fence. "Mom, do you think there's anything back there?" she asked, clutching a small flashlight.

Her mom smiled knowingly. "Why don't you find out, sweetie? Sometimes, the best adventures are hidden in the places we're too scared to explore."

Emma had always avoided that part of the yard. The tall grass and thorny vines made it look like a jungle, and she'd heard strange rustling noises there at night. But today, something inside her sparked—a mix of curiosity and determination.

"What if there's a snake or something?" Emma hesitated, looking back at her mom.

"Snakes don't usually hang out where people do. Besides, you've got your gloves and boots on. You'll be fine," her mom reassured her.

Armed with her flashlight, a pair of gardening gloves, and her mom's encouragement, Emma took her first step into the tangled greenery. At first, it was tough going. The vines snagged her gloves, and the tall grass brushed against her legs. She almost turned back, but then she spotted something shiny in the dirt. She knelt to pick it up and found an old key, its surface etched with swirling patterns.

"A key?" she whispered to herself. She held it up, watching it glint in the sunlight. "What could this open?"

As she pushed further into the bushes, her heart raced. After a few minutes, she stumbled upon something incredible: a small wooden door built into the base of an old tree. It was covered in moss and almost invisible among the roots. Emma's hands trembled as she tried the key. "It fits perfectly," she thought.

The door creaked open to reveal a hidden garden. Flowers of every color bloomed in wild patterns, and a tiny pond shimmered in the sunlight. Emma couldn't believe her eyes. She stepped inside, feeling like she had entered a storybook.

"Whoa," she said out loud, spinning in place to take it all in. "It's like a secret world!"

Exploring the garden, she found a wooden bench with carvings of animals on its surface and a small box tucked beneath it. Inside the box was a notebook filled with sketches of the garden and notes about its plants. The last entry read: "For the next explorer of this magical place—may you add your own discoveries to its story."

"The next explorer?" Emma wondered. "How long has this been here?"

She flipped through the notebook, marveling at the beautiful drawings of flowers, trees, and even small creatures that must have lived in the garden. She decided then and there to bring her sketchbook the next day and start documenting her adventures in the secret garden. The garden wasn't scary at all. In fact, it was the most wonderful place she'd ever seen.

That evening, Emma told her mom about her discovery. "I was so scared to go back there, but now I'm glad I did," she said over dinner.

Her mom smiled, knowing well what was in the garden. "Now you know that, sometimes, the best things are waiting just beyond your fears."

The next day, Emma invited her best friend Mia to see the garden. Mia was amazed. "Are you kidding me? This is like something out of a movie!"

"I know, right?" Emma said, leading her around. "Look at this pond—it's so clear. And check out the notebook I found!"

Together, they explored every corner, coming up with stories about how the garden had come to be. "Maybe it was made by fairies!" Mia suggested, pointing to a patch of tiny mushrooms.

"Or maybe a really old gardener who loved plants," Emma countered, examining the carvings on the bench.

The two girls spent hours in the garden, laughing, drawing, and even making up a secret handshake to celebrate their discovery.

Later that week, Emma decided to show her younger brother, Alex. "You can't tell anyone else, okay? It's our secret!" she told him.

"I won't, I promise!" Alex said, his eyes wide with excitement. "Wow, Emma, you're like a real explorer. I can't believe you found this!"

Alex's enthusiasm made Emma feel proud. "I guess I am kind of an explorer," she said with a grin.

Over time, the garden became Emma's special place. She brought new plants to add to the garden, hung a small wind chime on a tree branch, and even left her own notes in the notebook for future explorers to find.

One day, as she sketched a butterfly that had landed on a flower, Emma thought about how scared she'd been initially. "If I'd let my fear stop me, I never would have found this place," she said to herself.

What Emma Learned

Emma learned that facing fears can lead to incredible discoveries. The garden became her special place, a reminder that bravery isn't about being fearless—it's about being curious enough to take the first step.

Affirmation for Bravery

Write this affirmation in your diary and repeat it in your mind as you try something new:

"I am brave enough to take small steps, and I trust that amazing things are waiting for me."

Try This

1. Think of a place or activity you've avoided because it seemed too scary or difficult. Can you take one small step towards it?
2. Create a "Discovery Journal" where you write about new things you try or explore. Add sketches or photos to make it more fun.
3. Plan a "Courage Quest"! Choose one small challenge, like trying a new food or talking to someone new, and treat it like an adventure. Reflect on how you felt before and after; you may be surprised by your own bravery!

Emma's story reminds us that bravery opens the door to adventure. What will you discover next?

Chapter 2: Jamie and the Great Science Fair Challenge

Jamie sat at the dining table, her head buried in her hands. The flyer for the upcoming school science fair lay crumpled beside her. "I can't do this," she mumbled.

Her dad looked up from his laptop. "Why not? You love science. Remember the volcano experiment you did last year?"

"Yeah, but that was just for fun," Jamie sighed. "This is different. What if my project doesn't work? What if everyone laughs at me?"

Her dad set his coffee down and leaned forward. "Jamie, did you know Thomas Edison failed over a thousand times before he was able to invent the light bulb? He once said, 'I haven't failed. I've just found 10,000 ways that won't work.' Failure isn't the end; it's how you learn."

Jamie frowned, but deep down, she felt a flicker of inspiration. "Maybe," she said hesitantly. "But I don't even have an idea."

The next day at school, Jamie's best friend, Zoe, was bursting with excitement. "Guess what? I'm building a robot for the science fair! It's going to move and everything! What are you doing?"

"I don't know yet," Jamie admitted. "I'm afraid whatever I choose will flop."

Zoe tilted her head. "Even if it does, so what? My robot might not work either, but I'll have fun trying. You just need to pick something you're curious about."

Jamie considered what Zoe had said. That evening, she sat with her dad, flipping through a science book. "What about a solar-powered car?" he suggested. "You've always loved building things."

Jamie's eyes lit up. "That could be cool! But what if it doesn't work?"

"Then you'll learn what doesn't work," her dad said with a grin. "And that's just as important."

Over the next few weeks, Jamie worked tirelessly on her project. She watched videos about solar panels, drew sketches of her car design, and experimented with different materials. There were plenty of hiccups along the way. One afternoon, the motor wouldn't start, no matter what she tried. Frustrated, Jamie flopped onto the couch.

"I'm done," she declared. "This is a disaster."

Her mom sat beside her. "Jamie, what does success look like to you?"

Jamie shrugged. "A car that works."

Her mom smiled. "What about learning something new or having fun while you build it? Success isn't just about the final result. It's about the journey."

Jamie sighed but decided to give it another try. By the weekend, her car was almost ready. It wasn't perfect, but it moved—even if only a few inches at a time. And every small victory felt like a huge accomplishment.

The night before the science fair, Jamie couldn't sleep. "What if my car breaks during the presentation?" she asked her dad.

"Let's try something," he said. "Close your eyes and imagine everything going well. Picture yourself explaining your project confidently. Hear the applause at the end."

Jamie smiled, picturing the scene in her head. "That helps a little."

Her dad handed her a notebook. "Write down the steps you'll take tomorrow. Breaking things into small steps can make big challenges less scary."

Jamie wrote:

1. Set up the car.
2. Explain how solar power works.
3. Show the car moving.
4. Answer questions.

With her plan in place, Jamie finally felt ready.

At the science fair, Jamie's hands shook as she set up her project. But when it was her turn to present, she took a deep breath and began. "Hi, I'm Jamie, and this is my solar-powered car."

As she spoke, her confidence grew. The car didn't move perfectly, but it moved. The audience clapped, and a judge said, "Great work, Jamie. I love how you explained the science behind your project."

Afterwards, Zoe ran over. "You did it! Your car was awesome."

Jamie grinned. "It wasn't perfect, but I learned so much. I'm really glad I tried. Thank you to you, too."

What Jamie Learned

Jamie realized that failure isn't something to fear; it's a stepping stone to success. Every mistake taught her something new, and the journey was equally rewarding as the final success.

Affirmation for Courage

Write this affirmation in your diary and repeat it in your mind as you try something new:

"Every step I take, even if I stumble, brings me closer to success and new discoveries."

Try This

1. Think of a challenge you've been avoiding because you fear failing. Take one small step towards it today.
2. Write down a list of "failures" that taught you something valuable. Celebrate what you learned from them.
3. Pick a simple challenge (like juggling or drawing with your non-dominant hand) and enjoy the process, no matter the outcome!

Jamie's story reminds us that bravery isn't about never failing; it's about trying, learning, and growing. What will you try next?

Chapter 3: Ellie's Big Day at the Treehouse

Ellie stood at the base of the old oak tree, staring up at the treehouse. Her friends—Maya and Liam—were already at the top, waving down at her. "Come on, Ellie! The view is amazing!" Maya called out.

Ellie's palms felt clammy as she gripped the rope ladder. She wanted to climb; she really did, but the thought of being so high off the ground made her stomach churn. "I… I'll be up in a minute!" she shouted back, trying to sound brave.

Maya climbed halfway down to meet her. "You can do this, Ellie. Just take it one step at a time. I'll climb with you."

Liam chimed in from above, "Yeah, and if you fall, we'll catch you! Well, maybe not Maya—she's tiny—but I've got you!"

Ellie couldn't help but laugh. "Okay, okay. But if I scream, don't laugh at me!"

Ellie took a deep breath and placed one foot on the bottom rung of the rope ladder. The ladder wobbled slightly, and she froze.

10

"Just focus on this step," Maya said gently. "Don't think about the top yet."

Ellie nodded, her heart pounding. One step. Then another. Each time she moved, she repeated in her head, *I'm brave enough to do this.*

Halfway up, she paused to catch her breath. "How do you two make this look so easy?" she asked.

Maya shrugged. "We've had practice. It was scary for me the first time, too. But now it's fun!"

"And totally worth it!" Liam added. "Wait until you see the view."

Ellie reached the top rung and grabbed Maya's outstretched hand. "I made it!" she gasped, pulling herself onto the treehouse platform. The view took her breath away. From up here, she could see the entire neighborhood, the sparkling blue lake in the distance, and even the tops of other trees swaying in the breeze.

"It's beautiful," she whispered.

As they sat in the treehouse, Liam pulled out a bag of cookies. "For the bravest climber of the day!" he said, handing Ellie one.

"Thanks," Ellie said, smiling. "I couldn't have done it without you two."

"That's what friends are for," Maya said. "Remember last summer when I was scared to swim in the lake? You helped me then. Now it's your turn to be brave."

Ellie felt a warm glow. Having friends who believed in her made all the difference. "Maybe next time I'll climb up without hesitating," she said.

"Next time?" Liam teased. "Who are you, and what have you done with Ellie?"

They all laughed, and Ellie realized how much lighter she felt. Facing her fear had seemed impossible at first, but now she felt proud—and even a little excited—to try again.

Over the next few weeks, Ellie decided to take on more "micro-bravery challenges." She tried raising her hand in class, even when she wasn't sure her answer was correct. She practiced riding her bike down the steep hill near her house. And every evening, she wrote in her journal about the brave things she'd done that day.

One day, she saw a poster for the school talent show, and her heart skipped a beat. Although she loved playing guitar, she had never performed in front of an audience. Could she really do it?

"Why not?" she thought. "I climbed the treehouse. I can do this, too."

On the night of the talent show, Ellie stood backstage, clutching her guitar. Her hands trembled, and she felt a lump in her throat. "What if I mess up? What if they laugh?"

Maya and Liam were in the front row, waving and giving her two big thumbs up. Ellie took a deep breath and stepped onto the stage. She sat on the stool, adjusted the microphone, and began to play.

At first, her fingers fumbled on the strings, but as she got into the rhythm of the song, she forgot about the audience. She closed her eyes and let the music flow. When she finished, the room erupted into applause.

Ellie's face lit up as she took a bow. She felt unstoppable.

What Ellie Learned

Ellie learned that courage isn't about being fearless; it's about taking small steps and trusting yourself. With each challenge she faced, she grew braver and more confident. She realized that having a support system made challenges easier and that celebrating small victories helped her keep going.

Affirmation for Courage

Write this affirmation in your diary and repeat it in your mind as you try something new:

"I am brave enough to take small steps, and each step brings me closer to my dreams."

Try This

1. Create a "Bravery Journal" where you write down one brave thing you did each day. Celebrate your progress!
2. Surround yourself with friends or family who encourage you. Share your goals with them and ask for their support.
3. Practice visualizing success. Close your eyes and picture yourself doing the thing you're afraid of—and doing it well.

Ellie's story shows us that bravery is a skill we can all build, one step at a time. What's your next step towards courage?

Part 2: Unlocking the Confidence Code

Hi there, Confidence Builder!

Have you ever noticed how some people seem to glow with confidence? They may not always be the best at everything, but they believe in themselves, and that makes all the difference.

Here's the big secret: confidence isn't about being perfect—it's about trusting yourself and knowing you can handle whatever comes your way.

Are you ready to crack the Confidence Code? Let's go!

Chapter 4: Lily and the Secret Choir Audition

Lily sat on the edge of her bed, clutching the music sheet tightly. Her heart was racing, and her mind was filled with "what ifs." Tomorrow was the big day—auditions for the school choir. While Lily loved singing in her room or with her family, the idea of singing in front of a panel of judges made her stomach churn. "What if I mess up? What if they laugh at me?" she whispered to herself.

Just then, her mom peeked into the room knowingly. "Lily, you've been humming that song all week. You've got this. Just trust yourself."

"But what if I... you know, freeze?" Lily said, her voice shaky.

Her mom sat beside her. "Do you know what inner strength is?" she asked.

Lily shook her head. "Is it like being super strong? Because I'm pretty sure I'm not that."

Her mom smiled. "Inner strength isn't about lifting heavy things. It's about trusting yourself, even when you're scared. It's about moving forward even when your knees feel wobbly."

Lily thought about that as she drifted off to sleep, the music sheet still in her hands.

The next morning, Lily's best friend, Emma, met her at the bus stop. "Are you ready for the audition?" Emma asked, adjusting her backpack.

"Kind of," Lily admitted. "I mean, I've practiced a lot, but what if I make a mistake?"

Emma grinned. "Do you know TS forgot her lyrics once on stage? And Ade's mic didn't work during a performance? They just kept going. It's not about being perfect; it's about trying."

Lily smiled. "I guess if they can do it, I can at least try."

As they walked into school, the audition list on the bulletin board loomed ahead. Lily felt her heart skip a beat. Her name was right there, third from the top. She ran her fingers over the paper as if touching it would give her courage.

When Lily entered the music room for the audition, the air felt thick with nervous energy. Other kids were practicing their songs in hushed tones or tapping their feet anxiously.

"Next up, Lily Martinez," called Mrs. Allen, the choir director.

Lily's hands trembled as she stood up. She walked to the front of the room, clutching her music sheet like it was a life raft.

"Take a deep breath," Mrs. Allen said gently. "When you're ready."

Lily closed her eyes and imagined herself singing in her room, where she felt safe. She thought about all the times she had practiced and how much she loved the song. She took a deep breath and began to sing.

Her voice started soft but grew stronger with each note. She hit the high notes she had worried about and even added a little flourish at the end. When she finished, there was a moment of silence before Mrs. Allen smiled. "Beautifully done, Lily."

The other kids clapped, and Lily felt a warmth spread through her chest. She had done it. She had trusted herself, even when she was scared.

Later, as Lily and Emma sat under the tree during lunch, Lily couldn't stop smiling.

"See? You were amazing!" Emma said, giving her a playful nudge. "I knew you could do it."

"Thanks," Lily said. "But I think I learned something today."

"Oh? What's that?" Emma asked.

"Inner strength isn't about being fearless. It's about doing something even when you're scared," Lily explained. "Like speaking up for yourself or deciding to keep going when things get hard."

Emma nodded. "And it's about knowing you don't have to be perfect. You just have to try."

Lily looked at the clouds drifting lazily above them. "I think I want to audition for the solo part next time."

Emma's eyes widened. "Whoa! Go, Lily!"

Lily laughed. "Well, if TS and Ade can bounce back, I can at least try."

What Lily Learned

Lily discovered that inner strength is about believing in yourself, even when unsure. It's about taking that first step, trusting your abilities, and moving forward despite fear. Each small act of courage builds a foundation for greater confidence and resilience.

Affirmation for Inner Strength

Write this affirmation in your diary and repeat it in your mind as you try something new:

"I trust myself to take the first step, and every step after makes me stronger."

Try This

1. Keep a journal of moments when you showed inner strength. Write down what you did, how it felt, and why you're proud of yourself.
2. Look up stories of people who overcame challenges to inspire you. Share their stories with friends or family.
3. The next time you feel nervous, take a deep breath and visualize yourself succeeding. Imagine how good it will feel to accomplish your goal.

Lily's story reminds us that inner strength isn't about being perfect or fearless. It's about trying, trusting, and growing stronger with every step. What will you discover about your inner strength today?

Chapter 5: Maine and the Great Rock-Climbing Adventure

Maine stared up at the towering rock wall in front of her. The surface was dotted with colorful grips, each one leading higher and higher. At the very top was a small flag fluttering in the wind. "I... I don't think I can do this," Maine whispered, her heart pounding in her chest.

Her best friend, Ruby, nudged her playfully. "Come on, Maine! It's just a rock wall. You've climbed trees before, right?"

"Climbing trees is different," Maine said, eyeing the daunting height. "What if I slip? What if everyone laughs at me?"

Ruby crossed her arms and grinned. "Then you'll get back up and try again. Besides, I'll be right here cheering you on.

Maine took a deep breath. She wasn't sure she believed Ruby, but the idea of sitting on the sidelines while everyone else had fun didn't feel great either. "Okay," she said finally. "I'll give it a shot."

The instructor handed Maine a harness and helmet. "Safety first," she said with a kind smile. "You'll be strapped in securely, so even if you slip, you won't fall far."

As Maine tightened the straps on her harness, she thought about the things she was good at. She loved building LEGO towers and solving puzzles. Both required patience and focus. Maybe she could use those same skills to climb the wall.

"What are you most proud of?" Ruby asked, sensing Maine's hesitation.

"I built a LEGO castle with over 1,000 pieces last month," Maine said with a small smile. "It took forever, but I didn't give up."

"Exactly!" Ruby said. "If you can do that, you can climb this wall. Just take it one step at a time."

Maine nodded. She placed her foot on the first grip, then her hand on another. The grips felt firm under her fingers, and the harness gave her a sense of security. "Okay, here goes nothing," she muttered.

As Maine climbed higher, her confidence began to waver. The grips seemed farther apart, and the ground felt miles below. "I'm not good enough for this," she thought. "What if I'm too weak to make it to the top?"

"Hey, Maine!" Ruby called from the ground. "You're doing awesome! Just keep going."

Maine paused and closed her eyes. She took a deep breath and then reminded herself of what Ruby had said earlier. "I'm learning and growing every day," she whispered to herself. I can do this."

She opened her eyes and reached for the next grip. One by one, she climbed higher, focusing on her progress rather than how much farther she had to go.

When she slipped once, the harness caught her, and the instructor's encouraging voice steadied her. "Great recovery, Maine! You've got this!"

Near the top, Maine's arms ached, and her fingers felt like jelly. She glanced down and saw Ruby waving at her. "Almost there! You're so close!"

The flag was just a few grips away. Maine's legs trembled as she pushed herself upward. She gritted her teeth and grabbed the final grip, pulling herself to the top. When her hand touched the flag, a cheer erupted from below.

"You did it!" Ruby shouted, jumping up and down.

Maine grinned as she looked out over the climbing area. The view from the top was incredible, and the sense of accomplishment made every ache and fear worth it.

What Maine Learned

Maine learned that building inner strength starts with believing in yourself. By focusing on her progress and challenging the negative thoughts that held her back, she discovered that she could do more than she thought. Embracing discomfort and taking one step at a time helped her achieve something she once thought was impossible.

Affirmation for Inner Strength

Write this affirmation in your diary and repeat it in your mind as you try something new:

"I am strong, capable, and ready to face challenges one step at a time."

Try This

1. Write down three things you've accomplished that you're proud of. Think about how those strengths can help you face new challenges.
2. The next time you think, "I'm not good enough," replace it with, "I'm learning and growing every day."
3. Choose a small challenge that makes you a little nervous, like trying a new sport or speaking up in class. Celebrate your effort, no matter the outcome.

Maine's story shows us that inner strength isn't about never feeling scared or uncertain. It's about taking small, brave steps towards growth and discovering how capable you are. What will your next step be?

Part 3: Facing Your Fears

Hi there, Fearless Warrior!

Have you ever been so scared to try something new that it felt like your feet were glued to the ground? You're not alone! Fear can be really tough, but here's the thing: it's also a chance to grow. In this part of the book, we will talk about how to face those fears head-on—and maybe even use them as fuel to do something extraordinary.

This is just the beginning of something awesome. So, are you ready to take on your fears? Let's do it together!

Inspiring Stories for Amazing Girls Who Believe in Themselves

Chapter 6: Shanaya and the Mystery of the Forest Trail

Shanaya pulled her bike to a stop at the edge of the dense forest. She squinted at the path ahead, dappled with sunlight and shadow. In her backpack, she carried a crumpled map she'd drawn herself, marking the route to a hidden stream where her friends swore there were sparkling stones.

"You're sure you can find it?" her friend Kiran had asked earlier, raising an eyebrow.

"Of course!" Shanaya had said confidently. But now, staring at the winding trail, her confidence wavered.

The forest was quiet except for the occasional chirp of a bird. Shanaya adjusted her backpack straps and took a deep breath. "I can do this," she muttered, pushing her bike forward.

The path started easily enough, with clear signs pointing to different trails. But as Shanaya ventured deeper, the signs disappeared. Her map didn't match the twists and turns of the real forest. Soon, she found herself at a crossroads without knowing which way to go.

She tried the left path, but it led to a thicket of brambles. The right path led her to a stream—but not the one with sparkling stones. She slipped on a mossy rock and landed with a splash, soaking her shoes and pants. Frustrated, she sat on a boulder to catch her breath.

"Why did I think I could do this?" she whispered, fighting back tears. Memories of past failures crept into her mind: the time she'd fallen off her bike during a race, the science project that had toppled over during the fair. "I always mess up," she thought.

But then she remembered something her dad had told her: "Every mistake is just a step towards learning something new."

"Maybe this is just a lesson," she said aloud, brushing off her wet shoes. "It's okay not to get it right the first time."

As Shanaya made her way back to the main trail, she couldn't help but think about Kiran's earlier question. What if her friends laughed at her for not finding the stream? What if they thought she wasn't brave or smart?

She stopped and shook her head. "Who cares what they think?" she said firmly. "I tried, and that's what matters."

Shanaya decided to take a break at a small clearing. She pulled out a sandwich and her notebook, where she liked to sketch ideas and jot down thoughts. As she flipped through the pages, an idea struck her.

"What if I look for something new?" she wondered. "This forest must have other treasures."

Feeling lighter, she began walking along the trail, not worrying about maps or destinations. Her eyes scanned the trees, the ground, and the sky for anything interesting.

After a while, Shanaya spotted something unusual: a tree with carvings in its bark. She stepped closer and saw initials surrounded by a heart, along with a date from fifty years ago.

"Whoa," she whispered. "Someone was here a long time ago."

Curious, she followed the trail further and noticed more carved trees, each telling a small story. One had a bird drawing, and another had a poem. It felt like the forest was sharing its secrets with her.

Finally, she came across a wooden box hidden at the base of an old, rugged hut. Her heart raced as she opened it. Inside was a collection of tiny treasures: a feather, a polished stone, a little bottle with a note inside. The note read: *To those who seek, the forest always provides.*

Shanaya's disappointment about the stream melted away. She realized she'd found something even better—a hidden piece of history and a reminder of the magic in unexpected places.

What Shanaya Learned

Shanaya learned that failure isn't the end of the journey; it's just a step along the way. By letting go of her fear of judgment and embracing curiosity, she discovered something incredible. She realized that success isn't always about completing a task but about finding joy and meaning in the process.

Affirmation for Moving Forward

Write this affirmation in your diary and repeat it in your mind as you face new challenges:

"Every step I take, even if it leads somewhere unexpected, brings me closer to growth and discovery."

Try This

1. Think about a time you felt you "failed." Write down what you learned from the experience and how it helped you grow.
2. Try exploring a new place with your grown-ups or friends, like a park or trail, without a specific goal. Focus on noticing details and enjoying the journey.
3. Keep a journal of moments when you tried something new or overcame a fear, no matter the outcome.

Shanaya's story shows us that moving on from setbacks can lead to unexpected treasures. What new adventure will you embark on today?

Chapter 7: Zara and the Great Math Exam Adventure

Zara sat at her desk, staring at the brightly colored posters on the classroom wall. Her teacher, Ms. Patel, was explaining the rules for the upcoming math exam. Words like "algebra" and "geometry" floated through the air, but Zara's mind was stuck on one thought: *What if I fail?*

Math had never been Zara's favorite subject. Numbers swam before her eyes, twisting into impossible puzzles. Just thinking about the exam made her palms sweat. The only thing scarier than the test itself was imagining what her classmates might think if she messed up.

At recess, Zara sat under the big birch tree, doodling in her notebook. Her best friend, Lila, plopped down beside her. "Why so serious?"

"It's the math exam," Zara admitted. "I feel like I'm the only one who doesn't get it."

Lila tilted her head. "But you're really good at solving riddles. Remember that time you figured out the treasure hunt clue before anyone else?"

Zara shrugged. "That's different. Riddles are fun. Math is just... math."

"Maybe it's not so different," Lila said thoughtfully. "What if your fear is just pointing you towards something you're about to get better at?"

"What do you mean?" Zara asked.

"Ms. Patel always says fear is like a guide," Lila explained. "It shows you where you have room to grow. Maybe you're scared of math because it's something you're about to conquer."

Zara tapped her pencil against her notebook. Could fear really be a clue about where she had potential?

That evening, Zara sat at the kitchen table with her dad, who was reading the newspaper. "Dad, how do you know if something's scary because it's dangerous or just because it's new?"

Her dad put down his paper and smiled. "Great question, Zara. The danger is real, like crossing a busy street without looking both ways. Fear, though, is often about things we imagine might go wrong. Like, 'What if I trip in front of everyone?' Most of the time, those 'what ifs' don't come true."

"So, my math exam isn't dangerous," Zara said slowly, "but I'm still scared of messing up."

"Exactly," her dad said. "And the best way to deal with those fears is to face them head-on. What's the worst that could happen?"

"I guess I could get a few answers wrong," Zara said. "But I'm already practicing. And Ms. Patel says mistakes are just part of learning."

Her dad nodded. "Sounds like you're already on the right track."

The next day, Zara decided to take action. During math class, instead of hiding behind her book, she raised her hand. "Ms. Patel, can we go over the word problems again? I'm stuck on the last one."

Ms. Patel beamed. "Amazing, Zara! Let's work through it together."

As they solved the problem step by step, Zara realized she wasn't as lost as she'd thought. She just needed to break the problem into smaller parts—like solving a riddle.

That evening, Zara and Lila turned math practice into a game. They created their own silly word problems, like "If Lila eats three cupcakes and Zara eats five, how many cupcakes do they have left if a hungry dog steals two?"

"This is actually fun," Zara admitted, laughing.

"Told you!" Lila said, grinning.

On the morning of the exam, Zara's stomach churned with nervous energy. She clutched her lucky pencil as she sat at her desk. "It's just a piece of paper," she whispered to herself. "I've practiced, and I'm ready."

When Ms. Patel handed out the test, Zara took a deep breath and read the first question carefully. She worked through each problem step by step, just like they'd practiced. Some questions were tricky, but she didn't let herself panic.

By the time she reached the last question, Zara felt a sense of calm. She double-checked her answers and handed in her paper with a smile.

What Zara Learned

Zara learned that fear isn't the enemy—it's a guide. By facing her fear of math, she discovered that she just needed to practice and learn to solve. She realized that breaking big challenges into smaller steps made them less overwhelming, and asking for help was a sign of strength.

Affirmation for Facing Fear

Write this affirmation in your diary and repeat it in your mind as you face new challenges:

"I am brave enough to face my fears and smart enough to find solutions, one step at a time."

Try This

1. Write down something you're scared of. Then ask yourself: Is this a real danger or just a "what if" fear?
2. Take a big challenge and divide it into smaller, manageable tasks. Focus on completing one step at a time.
3. When you're stuck, reach out to a friend, teacher, or family member. Collaboration can make challenges feel easier.
4. No matter the outcome, reward yourself for trying and try again later. Every step forward is progress.

Zara's story reminds us that courage isn't about never feeling afraid—it's about taking action anyway. What fear will you face today?

Chapter 8: Maria and the Power of Self-Talk

Maria sat at her desk, nervously tapping her pencil against her history workbook. The teacher had just handed back the latest test results, and once again, her score was at the bottom of the page. She stared at the red number circled at the top, her heart sinking. *Why can't I ever get this right?* she thought.

Her classmates were chatting about their grades, comparing answers, and laughing. Maria wanted to disappear. She shoved the paper into her backpack and kept her head down for the rest of the day.

That evening, Maria's mom found her sitting on her bed, staring out the window. "Hey, sweetheart," she said gently, sitting down beside her. "Tough day?"

Maria nodded. "I'm just not good at school," she muttered. "No matter how hard I try, I always mess up."

Her mom frowned. "Maria, what's that voice in your head telling you right now?" Maria looked confused. "What do you mean?"

"Your inner voice," her mom explained. "The one that says, 'I'm not good enough' or 'I can't do this.' That's called self-talk. And sometimes, that voice can be really mean."

Maria thought for a moment. "Yeah, it's definitely mean. It's always saying things like 'You'll never get better' or 'Everyone else is smarter than you.'"

"That's negative self-talk," her mom said. "And it's not helping you. But here's the good news: you can change that voice."

Maria frowned. "How do I change it? It feels like it's always there."

"Well," her mom said, "imagine you're standing at the edge of a diving board. If you keep telling yourself, 'I'll fall,' you'll never jump. But if you say, 'I can do this,' you might surprise yourself. Negative thoughts actually trap us in a cycle of fear. They make us avoid trying, and we miss the chance to grow when we don't try."

Maria thought about the diving board at the community pool. She'd been too scared to try it all summer, even though she really wanted to. "So, if I tell myself I can do it, it might help?" she asked.

"Exactly," her mom said. "It takes practice, but positive self-talk is powerful. Let's start with your schoolwork. What if, instead of saying, 'I'll never get this,' you say, 'I'm learning, and I'll keep getting better'?"

The next day, Maria sat down at the kitchen table with her history workbook. Her mom joined her with a cup of tea. "Okay," Maria said, flipping to a tricky assignment. "Here's one I always mess up."

"What does your inner voice say?" her mom asked.

"It says, 'You'll never figure this out.'"

"Let's change that," her mom said. "Try saying, 'I'll take it step by step.'"

Maria hesitated, then repeated the words: "I'll take it step by step." She began recalling the incidents from that period of history by jotting them down as smaller points, and to her surprise, she discovered the answer. "I did it!" she exclaimed.

Her mom smiled. "See what happens when you change the way you talk to yourself?"

Maria felt a flicker of hope. Maybe her mom was right. Perhaps she could get better if she stopped being so hard on herself.

The following week, Maria's teacher announced a history quiz. Maria's stomach flipped. She could already hear her inner voice whispering, *You'll fail again.*

But then she remembered her mom's advice. "What if I succeed?" she whispered to herself. "What if this time is different?"

During the quiz, Maria took her time, repeating encouraging phrases in her mind: *I am capable. I can do this.* When she got stuck, she took deep breaths and reminded herself to focus on one sentence at a time.

When the teacher handed back the quizzes, Maria's hands shook. But when she saw her score, her eyes widened. She'd scored higher than she ever had before. "I did it!" she whispered.

Rose, who sat next to her, leaned over. "Wow, Maria! Great job!"

Maria beamed. For the first time, she felt proud of herself.

What Maria Learned

Maria learned that her inner voice has a powerful impact on how she feels and what she achieves. By replacing negative self-talk with positive affirmations, she discovered her ability to tackle challenges. She realized that mistakes are part of learning and that every step forward counts, no matter how small.

Affirmation for Positive Self-Talk

Write this affirmation in your diary and repeat it in your mind as you face new challenges:

"I am capable, I am learning, and I am growing stronger every day."

Try This

1. When you notice yourself thinking, "I can't," pause and replace it with, "I'll try."
2. Write down three positive statements about yourself and repeat them daily.
3. Share what you've learned about self-talk with someone else and cheer them on.

Maria's story reminds us that the way we talk to ourselves shapes what we believe we can do. What will you tell yourself today?

Part 4: Resilience: Bouncing Back Stronger

Hi there, Unstoppable Dreamer!

Let's talk about something super important: resilience. That's a fancy word for bouncing back when things don't go as planned. Have you ever felt like giving up after a big disappointment? Don't worry—we've all been there. But here's the good news: every challenge is a chance to grow stronger.

You must learn to get back up after falling down—and discover just how strong you really are. Are you ready to turn setbacks into comebacks? Let's get started!

Chapter 9: Laura and the Big Swim Challenge

Laura stood at the edge of the swimming pool, her toes curling over the cool tiles. The water shimmered in the early morning sunlight, but it looked less inviting and more intimidating to her today. She'd been training for weeks for the inter-school swimming competition, but her last practice had been a disaster.

What if I mess up again? she thought, her heart pounding.

Coach Emily clapped her hands, pulling Laura out of her thoughts. "Alright, team, let's run through the relay one more time! Laura, you're up first."

Laura swallowed hard. Her teammates, Mona, Sofia, and Grace, gave her encouraging smiles. "You've got this," Mona said. "Remember, just focus on your stroke."

But Laura wasn't so sure. The memory of slipping off the starting block during her last practice replayed in her mind like a bad movie.

That evening, Laura sat on her bed, fiddling with the ribbons from past swimming events. Her dad walked in, carrying two mugs of hot cocoa. "Tough practice?" he asked, handing her a mug.

Laura nodded. "I just keep thinking about all the ways I could mess up. What if I slip again? Or swim too slowly?"

Her dad sat beside her. "Do you know what resilience means?"

"Kind of," Laura said. "Isn't it like... bouncing back?"

"Exactly," her dad said. "Resilience is about how you respond when things don't go as planned. It's not about never failing; it's about getting back in the pool and trying again. It's like a muscle—the more you use it, the stronger it becomes."

Laura frowned. "But how do I stop thinking about my mistakes?"

Her dad smiled. "By using them to grow. Every swimmer—even the professionals—has experienced moments where things didn't go perfectly. What matters is how you learn from those moments."

The next day at practice, Laura decided to share her worries with Coach Emily. "I keep thinking about last time," she admitted. "What if I slip again?"

Coach Emily nodded. "That's a normal fear, Laura. But let's break it down. What happened when you slipped?"

"I got back up and kept swimming," Laura said, surprised at how steady her voice sounded.

"Exactly!" Coach Emily said. "That's resilience. You didn't give up. And remember, every time you face a challenge, you're building confidence for the next one."

Laura nodded, feeling a spark of determination. Maybe her dad and Coach Emily were right. She couldn't undo her mistakes, but she could decide how to respond to them.

As the week progressed, Laura focused on her mindset. Before practice, she spent a few minutes closing her eyes and visualizing herself diving flawlessly off the block and gliding through the water. This practice helped her feel calm and focused.

Coach Emily explained, "When you practice resilience, you're actually strengthening the problem-solving areas of your brain. It's like giving your brain a workout."

Laura also started keeping a small journal in her swim bag. After each practice, she wrote down one thing she did well and one thing she wanted to improve. Celebrating small wins like improving her flip turns or maintaining a steady rhythm felt good.

Finally, the day of the competition arrived. The pool was packed with cheering crowds and the sound of splashing water. Laura's team huddled together, wearing matching blue swimsuits and caps.

"Nervous?" Sofia asked, noticing Laura's fidgeting hands.

"A little," Laura admitted. "But I'm also ready. I've worked hard for this."

When it was time for the relay, Laura stepped onto the starting block. She took a deep breath and repeated the words she'd been practicing: *I'm ready. I've got this.* The whistle blew, and Laura dove in. The water enveloped her, calm and familiar. She focused on each stroke, her arms cutting through the water smoothly. When she reached the end of her lap and touched the wall, she looked up to see Mona diving in for the next leg of the relay.

By the time Grace finished the final lap, their team had come in third place. It wasn't the first, but to Laura, it felt like a victory. She'd faced her fear and done her best.

What Laura Learned

Laura discovered that resilience is not about avoiding mistakes or always succeeding. It's about how you bounce back and keep trying, even when things get tough. She discovered that by focusing on her growth and celebrating small victories, she could turn her fears into fuel for success.

Affirmation for Resilience

Write this affirmation in your diary and repeat it in your mind as you face new challenges:

" **I become stronger with every challenge I face, and I'm proud of how far I've come.**"

Try This

1. Close your eyes and imagine yourself overcoming a challenge. Imagine how amazing it would be to achieve your goal.
2. Share what you've learned about resilience with a friend or teammate and cheer them on.
3. Write down one thing you learned from a recent setback and how it helped you grow.

Laura's story reminds us that resilience is like a muscle—the more one uses it, the stronger it gets. What challenge will you tackle today?

Chapter 10: The Secret to Tina's Triumph

Tina slouched in her chair as her teacher, Mrs. Harper, made the big announcement.

"Class, the final exams are only four weeks away," Mrs. Harper said with a smile that didn't match the collective groan of the students. "This is your chance to show how much you've learned this year. Remember, preparation and effort are the keys to success!"

Tina's heart sank. Unlike her best friend Leah, who aced every test, Tina struggled to keep up. The thought of final exams felt like staring up at a mountain she had no idea how to climb.

At lunch, Leah tried to reassure her. "Tina, don't stress. We can study together! You'll do great."

But Tina wasn't so sure. "What if I fail? Everyone will think I'm dumb," she whispered.

"You're not dumb," Leah said firmly. "We'll figure it out together."

That evening, Tina's mom noticed her fidgeting with her homework. "What's on your mind, sweetheart?"

"The finals," Tina admitted. "I don't think I can do it, Mom."

Her mom sat down beside her. "You're thinking about what you can't do instead of what you can. Let's make a plan, step by step. You'll see how much you're capable of."

With her mom's help, Tina broke her study material into smaller chunks and set a schedule. At first, it felt overwhelming, but each day, she ticked off a little more. Still, doubts lingered. At school, classmates like Brandon bragged about how easy the exams would be for them. "You better step up, Tina," he teased. "No pressure or anything."

Tina laughed nervously but felt her chest tighten.

One week before the exams, disaster struck. Tina had spent hours studying her science notes, but when Leah quizzed her, she froze. "I'll never get this," Tina groaned.

Leah tilted her head thoughtfully. "Remember that time I burned those cupcakes?"

Tina snorted. "Yeah, you turned them into charcoal muffins."

"Exactly! But then I tried again, and the second batch was perfect. Mistakes are just part of the process. It's like practice. You learn by doing it wrong first."

Tina considered this. Maybe failing a practice quiz didn't mean she was doomed; it meant she was learning.

For the next few days, Tina shifted her mindset. Instead of saying, "I can't do this," she told herself, "I'm not there yet, but I'm improving." She tackled her notes like a puzzle, piece by piece. Leah and her mom cheered her on, but Tina began to notice something even more important—she was cheering herself on, too.

When exam day finally arrived, Tina felt nervous but prepared. She walked into the classroom, sat at her desk, and took a deep breath.

A week later, Mrs. Harper handed back the graded exams. Tina's hands shook as she opened her science paper. Her eyes widened.

"85%!" she whispered. She had done it.

"Tina!" Leah grinned. "I told you!"

Brandon looked over, clearly impressed. "Guess you stepped up after all," he said with a grin.

Tina smiled. For the first time, she believed it too. It wasn't about being perfect but about giving her best and trusting the process.

What Tina Learned

Tina learned that resilience isn't about avoiding mistakes or being flawless. It's about believing in your ability to improve and seeing challenges as opportunities to grow. Mistakes are stepping stones, not roadblocks.

Affirmation for Courage

Write this affirmation in your diary and repeat it in your mind as you try something new:

"I am capable of learning and growing with every challenge I face."

Try This

1. When you find yourself thinking, "I can't," replace it with, "I'm not there yet, but I'm improving."
2. Write down a mistake you've made recently and what you learned from it. Celebrate the lesson.

3. Break a big challenge into smaller, manageable tasks. Focus on completing one step at a time.

Tina's journey shows that success isn't about perfection but courage, curiosity, and never giving up. What mountain will you climb next?

Chapter 11: Eliza and the Garden of Perseverance

Eliza knelt in her backyard, staring at the bare patch of dirt in front of her. In her hand, she held a small packet of sunflower seeds her grandmother had given her. "These are special seeds," Grandma had said with a wink. "They'll grow tall and strong if you take care of them. But they'll need patience and love."

Eliza had never planted anything before, but she was excited to try. She wanted to surprise her grandmother with a garden full of bright, golden sunflowers. But as she pressed the seeds into the soil, doubt crept into her mind. *What if they don't grow? What if I mess this up?*

The first week of gardening felt magical. Eliza watered her seeds daily, imagining the big flowers they'd become. But by the second week, nothing had sprouted. She began to worry. "Maybe I did something wrong," she told her mom one evening.

Her mom smiled. "Do you remember what Grandma told you? Plants take time. You must keep going, even when you can't see results yet. Just like the great achievements of so many brave people."

"Like who?" Eliza asked, curious.

"Well, think of a young girl who stood up for education despite facing immense challenges," her mom said. "She never gave up on her dream, no matter the obstacles. Or a writer who kept working on her book even after multiple rejections from publishers. They persevered, even when things got tough."

Eliza nodded, inspired. "So, I just have to keep trying?"

"Exactly," her mom said. "Great things take time and perseverance."

By the third week, Eliza's excitement had faded. The patch of dirt looked just as plain as it had on day one. Frustrated, she flopped down on the grass. "Maybe I should just stop," she muttered.

Her dad came outside and sat next to her. "What's wrong?"

"Nothing's growing," Eliza said, tears stinging her eyes. "I'm wasting my time."

Her dad thought for a moment. "Do you know what trees do during a storm?"

Eliza frowned. "What do you mean?"

"They bend," her dad said. "They don't try to fight the wind. They rest and wait for the storm to pass. But they don't give up. Sometimes, perseverance means taking a break, not quitting. You've been working hard, Eliza. Maybe it's time to rest and let nature do its part."

Eliza considered his words. "So, resting isn't the same as giving up?"

Her dad nodded. "Exactly. It's part of the process."

The next morning, Eliza watered her garden again. She decided to stop worrying about the results and just enjoy the process. She noticed the birds chirping in the trees and how the sunlight warmed her face. As she looked around, she realized how much nature could teach her. Trees stood tall despite storms, and rivers carved through rocks, flowing steadily over time.

A few days later, Eliza saw something that made her gasp. Tiny green shoots were poking through the soil. "They're growing!" she shouted, running inside to tell her family.

Her grandmother beamed when Eliza showed her the little sprouts. "I told you they were special," Grandma said. "And so are you, Eliza. You didn't give up. That's what made the difference."

Eliza's plants grew taller each week. She learned to pull weeds, protect them from bugs, and even added a little fence around her garden. By the end of summer, the sunflowers were taller than she was, and their yellow faces turned towards the sky.

What Eliza Learned

Eliza learned that perseverance doesn't mean everything will always go smoothly. It means continuing to care and try, even when results take time. She realized that resting isn't quitting; it's part of growing stronger. She discovered that nature has incredible lessons to teach—like how storms pass, rivers flow, and seeds grow into something beautiful with patience and love.

Affirmation for Perseverance

Write this affirmation in your diary and repeat it in your mind as you face new challenges:

"I will keep trying, even when it's hard, because every step brings me closer to my goal."

Try This

1. Choose something that takes time, like growing a plant or building a model. Celebrate every small step you complete.
2. Spend time outside and notice how plants and animals adapt to challenges. Write down what inspires you.
3. If you feel frustrated or stuck, take a break. Remind yourself that resting isn't the same as giving up.

Eliza's story reminds us that great things take time and effort, but the results are always worth it. What will you grow today?

Part 5: Compassion and Connection

Hi there, Kindness Champion!

Here's a little secret: the strongest people aren't just brave or tough—they're kind, too. Kindness possesses its superpower. It helps us connect with others, spread joy, and make the world a better place. And guess what? It feels amazing to be kind.

Compassion can change your life—and the lives of people around you. Are you ready to unleash your kindness superpower? Let's go!

Chapter 12: Ava and the Kindness Challenge

Ava was sitting on her bed, flipping through a colorful magazine, when an article caught her attention. The title read: "How One Girl Changed Her Community with a Kindness Challenge." Ava's eyes widened as she read about a girl who encouraged her classmates to perform random acts of kindness, spreading joy throughout her town. The story ended with a powerful line: *Kindness is contagious. You never know how far one small act can go.*

Ava closed the magazine and stared out her bedroom window. She'd always wanted to make a difference but didn't know where to start. Could she do something like that?

The next day at school, Ava couldn't stop thinking about the article. At lunch with her best friends, Maya and Jayden, she shared the idea.

"A kindness challenge?" Maya asked, raising an eyebrow. "How would that work?"

"We could start by doing small things for people," Ava explained. "Like holding the door open or writing thank-you notes. If everyone joins in, it could grow into something really big."

Jayden grinned. "I like it. Kindness ninjas! Sneaky, but with good intentions."

Maya laughed. "Okay, I'm in. Let's see how many people we can get to join us."

Ava felt a flutter of excitement. They decided to start small with a challenge for their class: one kind act a day for a week.

On the first day of the challenge, Ava wrote a thank-you note to her teacher, Mrs. Carter. She slipped it onto her desk before class started. When Mrs. Carter read the note, her face lit up. "Thank you, Ava. This made my day."

Seeing Mrs. Carter's smile brought Ava a warm feeling in her chest. She recognized how impactful even a small gesture could be.

Maya helped a younger student carry a heavy art project to the bus, and Jayden surprised the janitor with a cup of coffee. By the end of the day, their classmates started noticing.

"What's going on with you three?" Ellie asked as they packed up their backpacks.

"We're doing a kindness challenge," Ava said. "You should join us!"

Ellie shrugged but smiled. "Maybe."

The next day, Ellie brought cookies for everyone at her lunch table. Word spread quickly, and soon, more students were participating. By the end of the week, the whole class was buzzing with stories of kind acts: helping with homework, leaving encouraging notes, and even surprising the bus driver with a thank-you card.

At the end of the week, Ava's class held a special meeting to share their experiences. One by one, her classmates stood up to talk about how the kindness challenge had affected them.

"I didn't think it would be a big deal," Ellie admitted, "but seeing everyone's smiles made me so happy."

"Same here," Jayden said. "When I gave the janitor that coffee, he said it was the nicest thing anyone had done for him all week. It felt good to make his day."

Ava beamed as she listened. The challenge had grown into something bigger than she'd imagined. Her teacher, Mrs. Carter, stood up and said, "This challenge shows how small acts can create a ripple effect. You've all inspired me, and I hope you'll keep spreading kindness beyond this week."

What Ava Learned

Ava learned that kindness doesn't have to be grand to make a big impact. Every small act of compassion creates ripples, inspiring others to do the same. She discovered that kindness connects people, brightens days, and brings a sense of joy and purpose.

Affirmation for Kindness

Write this affirmation in your diary and repeat it in your mind as you look for ways to spread kindness:

"Every act of kindness, no matter how small, makes the world a better place."

Try This

1. Encourage your friends or family to join you in doing one kind act a day for a week.
2. Pick someone who's made a difference in your life and write them a heartfelt note of gratitude.

3. At the end of each day, write down how your kind act made you feel and how it might have affected the other person.

Ava's story reminds us that kindness is a superpower we all have. What act of kindness will you start with today?

Chapter 13: Dahlia and the Friendship Circle

Dahlia sat on the bench near the playground, watching the other kids laugh and play. In the corner of the field, a group of girls huddled together, giggling as they passed around a glittery notebook. It was the "Star Club," the most exclusive group in school. Dahlia had always wanted to join, but when she'd asked last year, they told her, "Sorry, we're full."

Today, though, she wasn't going to let that memory sting. She picked up her sketchbook and started doodling. "I don't need a club to have fun," she muttered, though her heart ached for belonging.

Later that afternoon, Dahlia went to the library. It was her favorite place, filled with the scent of old books and the quietness of creativity. She found her usual spot by the big window and opened her sketchbook.

"That's amazing!" a voice said. Dahlia looked up to see a boy her age, his glasses slipping down his nose. "Did you draw that?"

Dahlia nodded, blushing. "Yeah. I love drawing."

"Me too," the boy said, pulling out his sketchbook. "I'm Oliver."

They spent the next hour sharing their sketches. Dahlia learned that Oliver loved drawing comics, and she showed him her collection of fantasy illustrations. By the time they packed up, they'd decided to meet at the library every Wednesday to draw together.

The following week, Oliver brought his friend Priya, who loved painting landscapes. Dahlia introduced them to her classmate Nia, who wrote poetry. "We should start a group," Dahlia suggested. "A creative club for anyone who loves art, writing, or anything imaginative."

"That sounds awesome!" Priya said. "Let's do it."

The "Imagination Circle" was born. Every week, more kids joined—some sketched, some wrote, and others just came to share ideas and cheer each other on. Dahlia felt a warmth in her chest as she watched everyone encouraging one another.

"Your poem is beautiful," Dahlia told Nia one day. "It made me feel like I was walking through a magical forest."

"Thanks," Nia said, beaming. "And your dragon drawing... wow. It looks like it could fly off the page."

When Priya struggled to find the perfect shade of blue for her painting, Oliver offered tips. "Try adding a little white," he suggested. "It'll make it pop."

"You're a genius," Priya said, laughing.

Each meeting was filled with laughter, ideas, and unspoken promises about having each other's backs.

One rainy afternoon, Dahlia noticed a girl sitting alone at the edge of the library. She looked shy, her hands tucked into her sleeves as she watched the Imagination Circle from afar.

Dahlia walked over. "Hi, I'm Dahlia. Do you like art or writing?"

The girl hesitated, then nodded. "I like writing stories. But I'm not very good."

"Everyone starts somewhere," Dahlia said with a smile. "Why don't you join us? We'd love to hear your stories."

The girl, Lila, joined hesitantly but soon felt at home. The group cheered when she read her first story aloud, and by the end of the meeting, Lila was laughing and sharing ideas like she'd been part of the group forever.

Dahlia felt a sense of pride. She remembered how lonely she'd felt watching the Star Club and realized she'd built something even better—a place where everyone was welcome.

What Dahlia Learned

Dahlia learned that finding your tribe means looking for people who share your values and passions. By creating the Imagination Circle, she discovered the joy of supporting and being supported by others. She realized that kindness and inclusion could turn strangers into friends and that true belonging comes from building connections, not exclusivity.

Affirmation for Building Your Tribe

Write this affirmation in your diary and repeat it in your mind as you create connections:

"I welcome friendship and creativity, and together we can achieve amazing things."

Try This

1. Find a club or activity around you that matches your interests, or start one like Dahlia did.

2. Invite someone new to join your group. You might make their day or even become a lifelong friend.
3. Compliment a friend's work or cheer them on. Small gestures make a big difference.

Dahlia's story reminds us that friendship is about creating a space where everyone feels valued, loved, and supported. Who will you invite into your circle today?

Part 6: Dream Big, Act Boldly

Hi there, Big Dreamer!

What would you do if you weren't afraid? Think about it for a second. Dreaming big is amazing, but here's the real magic—it's about taking those dreams and turning them into reality. That takes boldness, a little courage, and a whole lot of belief in yourself.

Dreaming big is just the first step. Acting boldly? That's where the real magic happens. Let's dream big and act boldly together!

Chapter 14: Maggie and the Power of Big Dreams

Maggie sat cross-legged on her bed, a notebook resting on her lap. The pages were filled with sketches of robots, plans for apps, and ideas for inventions. She had always been fascinated by how things worked, taking apart old gadgets and trying to put them back together—sometimes successfully, sometimes not. But her biggest dream was to create something that could make the world better.

"Maggie," her mom called from the kitchen, "dinner's ready!"

"Coming!" Maggie shouted, closing her notebook. She placed it carefully under her pillow as though her dreams were too precious to leave in the open.

At dinner, her older brother, Ryan, asked, "What were you scribbling in that notebook of yours?"

Maggie blushed. "Just some ideas."

"Ideas for what?" her dad asked, curious.

Maggie hesitated, then took a deep breath. "I want to design an app that helps kids find fun ways to learn math. I know many kids struggle with it, and I think I can make it easier and more enjoyable."

Her family looked at her with admiration. "That's a great idea," her mom said. "Dreaming big is how great things start."

"Yeah," Ryan added, "but big dreams also take a lot of work. Are you ready for that?"

Maggie nodded firmly. "I'm ready."

The next day at school, Maggie shared her idea with her best friend, Tara. "That sounds amazing!" Tara said. "But how are you going to make an app? Do you even know how to code?"

"Not yet," Maggie admitted. "But I can learn."

Tara grinned. "I'll help you. Let's start by looking up free coding tutorials after school."

Maggie felt a surge of excitement. Her dream suddenly felt closer, like it wasn't just a far-off idea but something she could actually achieve.

That evening, Maggie and Tara sat in front of Maggie's computer, watching a beginner's coding video. At first, the lines of code looked like a foreign language. Maggie's head spun as the instructor explained variables and loops.

"This is harder than I thought," Maggie said, slumping back in her chair.

"Hey," Tara said, "remember what your mom said about big dreams? They start with small steps. Let's focus on learning small."

Maggie nodded. She spent the next hour practicing simple commands until she finally got a virtual balloon to move across the screen. "I did it!" she cheered.

"See?" Tara said. "You're already on your way."

Before bed that night, Maggie pulled out her notebook and sketched what her app might look like. She imagined kids laughing as they solved math problems disguised as fun challenges. She pictured herself presenting her app to a group of teachers and students, showing them how it worked.

Her mom peeked into her room. "What are you doing?"

"Visualizing," Maggie said with a smile. "I read that picturing success helps your brain get ready to make it happen."

Her mom beamed. "That's true. Your brain starts working towards the goals you set for yourself. Keep going, Maggie. You're doing great."

Over the next few weeks, Maggie worked tirelessly. She balanced coding practice with homework, often staying up late to tweak her designs. There were moments of frustration when the code didn't work or her ideas felt too big to handle. But she kept going, reminding herself why she started.

One day, during lunch at school, she overheard a classmate, Ben, complaining about how hard math was. Maggie hesitated, then walked over. "I'm working on an app to make math more fun," she said. "Would you want to test it when it's ready?"

Ben looked surprised but intrigued. "Sure. If it's fun, I'm in."

Maggie's heart swelled with pride. Her dream was starting to feel real.

After months of work, Maggie's app was ready for its first test. She invited Tara, Ben, and a few other friends to her house to try it out. As they played through the math games, their laughter filled the room.

"This is actually fun," Ben said, grinning. "I never thought I'd say that about math."

Maggie felt a surge of accomplishment. Her dream had started as a sketch in her notebook, but now it was something that could help others.

What Maggie Learned

Maggie learned that while big dreams might initially feel overwhelming, breaking them into small steps makes them achievable. She discovered that perseverance, curiosity, and asking for help are essential to turning dreams into reality. Most importantly, she realized that dreams not only shape one's future but also inspire and help others along the way.

Affirmation for Dreaming Big

Write this affirmation in your diary and repeat it in your mind as you work towards your goals:

"I have the power to dream big and take small steps to make my dreams come true."

Try This

1. Close your eyes and imagine what success looks like. What steps can you take to get there?
2. Write your big dream at the top of a page, then list smaller steps to work towards it.
3. Take the first step by learning a skill related to your dream, like coding, painting, or writing.

Maggie's story reminds us that big dreams start with small actions and grow through determination and courage. What big dream will you start working on today?

Chapter 15: Aurora and the Black Belt Quest

Aurora's heart pounded as she stepped into the dojo. The smell of sweat and polished wooden floors filled the air, and the rhythmic slap of feet against mats echoed around her. Tonight was her first advanced karate class, and though she'd dreamed of earning a black belt for years, a knot of fear sat heavy in her stomach.

"Aurora, are you ready?" Sensei Tanaka asked, his kind but piercing eyes meeting hers.

Aurora nodded, even though she wasn't sure. "I'll try," she said softly.

The class began with warm-ups, but Aurora's mind was elsewhere. What if she wasn't strong enough or fast enough? She glanced at the older students, their movements sharp and confident. How could she ever match them?

After class, Aurora lingered behind, staring at the wall of belts displayed proudly at the front of the dojo. Sensei Tanaka approached her. "Aurora, do you know what the black belt represents?"

"Being the best?" she guessed.

He smiled. "No. It represents perseverance. Every black belt was once a white belt that didn't give up, even when it felt like failing. Failure isn't the end—it's part of the journey."

Aurora thought about this as she walked home. Maybe failing didn't mean she wasn't good enough. Maybe it just meant she was learning.

The next week, Aurora's class focused on sparring. Paired with a more experienced student, she hesitated with every move. "You have to commit," her partner said. "If you don't believe in your kicks, neither will I."

That night, Aurora sat on her bed, staring at her karate journal. She'd written down every move she needed to master, but next to each one, her notes were filled with doubts: *I'm too slow. I'll never get this right.*

Her older brother, Ethan, peeked into her room. "What's up?" he asked.

"I'm not sure I can do this," Aurora admitted, showing him the journal.

Ethan read it and shook his head. "Why are you focusing on what you can't do? Start writing what you're going to try instead."

Aurora grabbed a fresh page and wrote, "I'll practice my roundhouse kick 10 times tomorrow. I'll focus on one step at a time." It felt like a slight shift, but she felt lighter as she closed the journal.

At school, Aurora's friends teased her about how much time she spent at the dojo. "Why do you even care about karate so much?" one of them asked. "It's not like you're going to the Olympics."

Aurora's cheeks burned. "It's important to me," she said, though her voice wavered.

Later, she confided in her mom. "Why can't people just be supportive?"

Her mom hugged her. "Not everyone will understand your dreams, Aurora, and that's okay. What matters is that *you* believe in them. Surround yourself with people who lift you up, like Sensei Tanaka and your brother. They're your team."

Feeling encouraged, Aurora decided to focus on the voices that mattered. With Ethan's help, she spent the next week practicing, turning her doubts into determination.

Finally, the day of the black belt test arrived. The dojo was filled with students, parents, and instructors. Aurora's hands trembled as she adjusted her uniform. The test was long and grueling, filled with sparring rounds, complex katas, and moments where she felt like giving up.

During one sparring match, Aurora was knocked down hard. She gasped for breath, her eyes stinging with tears. For a moment, she considered staying down. But then she heard Sensei Tanaka's voice in her head: *Every black belt was once a white belt who didn't give up.*

Aurora pushed herself up, steadying her stance. She met her opponent's gaze and continued the match, finishing strong.

When the test ended, the students lined up, waiting for the results. Sensei Tanaka called Aurora's name. "Step forward," he said, holding a black belt in his hands. Aurora's heart raced as he tied it around her waist. "You earned this," he said. "Not because you were perfect, but because you never gave up."

What Aurora Learned

Aurora learned that big dreams often come with challenges, but embracing those challenges makes success even sweeter. She discovered that failure isn't the end—it's a stepping stone to growth. By replacing limiting beliefs with determination and focusing on the support of those who believed in her, she achieved her dream of earning a black belt.

Affirmation for Courage and Perseverance

Write this affirmation in your diary and repeat it in your mind as you face new challenges:

"I am strong, determined, and capable of achieving my dreams, one step at a time."

Try This

1. Write down one fear that's holding you back and one step you can take to face it.
2. Surround yourself with friends, family, or mentors who encourage and inspire you.
3. Keep track of small victories, whether mastering a new skill or simply not giving up.

Aurora's journey shows us that dreams are worth pursuing, even when they seem tough. What dream will you chase today?

Chapter 16: Victoria and the Bold School Club

Victoria sat at her desk, doodling in the margins of her notebook. Her teacher was talking about Earth Day, and while the topic fascinated her, Victoria couldn't stop thinking about the amount of litter she'd seen in the park over the weekend. Wrappers, bottles, and even an old shoe had turned her favorite green space into an eyesore.

"What can we do about it?" she muttered to herself.

Her best friend, Ellie, leaned over. "What did you say?"

"The litter in the park," Victoria said, louder this time. "It's terrible! I wish we could fix it."

Ellie shrugged. "Yeah, it's bad, but what can we do? We're just kids."

But Victoria wasn't convinced. Maybe there was something she could do… if only she could figure out how.

That evening, Victoria sat at the kitchen table with a notebook, brainstorming ideas.

"What are you up to?" her dad asked, setting a plate of cookies in front of her.

"I want to clean up the park," Victoria said. "But it feels too big. What if nobody wants to help?"

Her dad smiled. "Acting boldly doesn't mean you're fearless. It means you're willing to take the first step, even when you're scared. Start first and see where it leads."

Victoria nodded, a spark of determination lighting in her eyes. "Okay. I'll start by asking my teacher if we can start a school club to clean up the park."

The next day, Victoria raised her hand during class. "Ms. Rivera, can I share an idea?" she asked, her voice trembling slightly.

"Of course, Victoria," Ms. Rivera said.

"I'd like to start a school club to help clean up the park," Victoria said. "We could call it the Green Team. Would that be okay?"

Ms. Rivera beamed. "What a wonderful idea! Let's make it happen."

Victoria created posters for the Green Team and hung them around the school. She felt nervous as she taped the first one to the bulletin board. "What if nobody signs up?" she whispered to Ellie.

"They will," Ellie said confidently. "And I'll be the first member."

By the end of the week, ten students had signed up for the Green Team. Their first meeting was filled with chatter and excitement as they planned their first cleanup event. Victoria stood at the front of the room, feeling a mix of pride and anxiety. "Thank you all for coming," she said. "Together, we can make the park beautiful again."

Each small step—putting up a poster, talking to her classmates, and leading the meeting—helped Victoria build confidence. She realized that boldness didn't have to mean grand gestures. It could start with something as simple as sharing an idea.

On the day of the cleanup, the Green Team gathered at the park with gloves, trash bags, and plenty of enthusiasm. As they worked, passersby stopped to watch and even offered to help. By the end of the day, the park looked clean and inviting.

A local reporter who had noticed the group approached Victoria. "This is impressive," she said. "Would you like to share your story for the newspaper?"

Victoria hesitated, then nodded. "Sure. I think it's important to show that kids can make a difference, too."

The article was published the following week, and soon, other schools reached out to start their own Green Teams. Victoria even received a call from a local business offering to sponsor future cleanup events. She couldn't believe how much had come from her small, bold idea.

What Victoria Learned

Victoria learned that bold actions, no matter how small, can create ripple effects of change. She discovered that acting boldly doesn't mean being fearless; it means taking the first step despite your fears. Most importantly, she realized that big dreams require courage, teamwork, and persistence to come to life.

Affirmation for Boldness

Write this affirmation in your diary and repeat it in your mind as you take steps toward your dreams:

"I am brave enough to take the first step, and every step brings me closer to making a difference."

Try This

1. Think of a dream or idea you've been hesitant about. Write down the first action you can take today to start.

2. Tell a friend, teacher, or family member about your idea. Their encouragement might give you the confidence to move forward.
3. Share your story to encourage others to act boldly and pursue their dreams.

Victoria's story reminds us that change starts with one brave step. What bold action will you take today?

Part 7: The Role of Gratitude

Hi there, Gratitude Genie!

Have you ever noticed how good it feels when you say "thank you" or when someone shows you kindness? Gratitude has a way of making everything feel brighter. But did you know it can also make you stronger, happier, and more confident?

A grateful heart is a powerful one. Let's dive in and discover the magic of gratitude!

Chapter 17: Isabella and the Gratitude Adventure

Isabella sat cross-legged on her bedroom floor, flipping through the pages of her travel scrapbook. She loved capturing memories of family trips to the beach, picnics at the park, and that one time her little brother accidentally wore two different shoes to a wedding. Each picture made her smile, but today, the scrapbook felt different. She sighed and closed it.

Her mom peeked into the room. "What's wrong, Bella? You usually love looking at those."

"I don't know," Isabella said, shrugging. "It's just... I've looked at these pictures a hundred times. Nothing feels exciting anymore."

Her mom sat down beside her. "Do you know what might help? Gratitude."

"Gratitude?" Isabella asked, raising an eyebrow. "Isn't that just saying thank you?"

"It's more than that," her mom said with a smile. "Gratitude is about noticing and appreciating the good things in your life—even the little ones. Let's turn today into a gratitude adventure."

As they sat on the porch next to Isabella's bedroom, sipping lemonade, her mom explained. "Gratitude means recognizing the good around us and being thankful for it. It's like finding hidden treasures in your day. Even challenges can teach us lessons worth appreciating."

Isabella frowned. "But how do you find gratitude when nothing exciting happens?"

Her mom grinned. "That's the fun part. You'll need a journal, sharp eyes, and a curious heart. Ready?"

Isabella nodded, feeling a flicker of excitement. "Okay. Where do we start?"

First, they headed to the park. Isabella's mom handed her a small notebook and pen. "Write down three things you notice that make you happy or thankful."

Isabella scanned the park. A little boy giggled as he blew bubbles. A dog wagged its tail furiously as its owner tossed a ball. A pair of robins chirped in a tree. She scribbled quickly.

"What did you write?" her mom asked.

"The bubbles, the happy dog, and the birds," Isabella said. "I didn't think about it before, but those things are kind of nice."

Her mom nodded. "That's gratitude at work. Did you know that practicing gratitude actually rewires your brain? It makes you focus on the positive, which helps you feel happier and less stressed."

Isabella grinned. "So, it's like a brain workout for feeling good?"

"Exactly," her mom said.

As the day went on, Isabella became a gratitude detective. At lunch, she noticed how the sun made the dining room warm and cozy. She thanked her dad for making her favorite grilled cheese sandwich. When her little brother drew her a wobbly stick-figure portrait, she smiled and said, "Thanks, Joey. I love it."

Later, they walked to the library. Isabella's mom pointed out a colorful mural on the wall. "What do you think of that?"

"It's beautiful," Isabella said, snapping a picture. She jotted down: *Grateful for art that makes the world prettier.*

At bedtime, Isabella's mom asked, "How was your gratitude adventure?"

"It was fun," Isabella said, flipping through her notebook. "I found so many little things to be thankful for. I never really noticed them before."

"That's the magic of gratitude," her mom said, tucking her in. "It helps you see the good that's always been there."

What Isabella Learned

Isabella learned that gratitude is more than just saying thank you. It's about noticing and appreciating the small joys in everyday life. She discovered that practicing gratitude made her feel happier and helped her see the world in a more positive light. Even on ordinary days, she found extraordinary moments.

Affirmation for Gratitude

Write this affirmation in your diary and repeat it in your mind as you reflect on your day:

"I am grateful for the small joys in life, and I choose to see the good around me."

Try This

1. Write down three things in your gratitude journal you're thankful for each day. They can be as simple as a kind word or a sunny afternoon.

2. Take a walk and notice things that make you smile or feel happy. Reflect on them afterward.
3. Turn gratitude into art! Each day, draw or doodle something you're thankful for in a notebook. By the end of the month, you'll have a colorful collection of happy memories to look back on!

Isabella's story reminds us that gratitude is like a treasure map, leading us to the joys hidden in everyday life. What treasures will you find today?

Chapter 18: Nora and the Power of Gratitude

Nora swung her backpack onto her shoulder, ready to head out of the classroom. She noticed her best friend, Ebony, sitting at her desk with her head down. Ebony hadn't said a word since their science teacher handed back the exam results.

"Ebony, are you okay?" Nora asked, kneeling beside her.

Ebony sniffled. "I failed. I studied so hard, and I still failed. I'm never going to be good at science."

Nora frowned. Ebony was usually cheerful and confident. Seeing her like this made Nora's heartache. She wanted to help but wasn't sure how.

"Come on," Nora said, gently tugging Ebony's arm. "Let's talk."

That evening, Nora sat at her desk, brainstorming ways to cheer Ebony up. Her mom walked in with a plate of cookies. "You look deep in thought," she said.

Nora explained what had happened. "I just want Ebony to feel better," she said. "She's always helping everyone else. How can I remind her how amazing she is?"

Her mom smiled. "Have you ever written her a thank-you note? Sometimes, hearing how much someone appreciates you can lift your spirits."

Nora grabbed a colorful notecard and started writing:

Dear Ebony, Thank you for always being such a kind and supportive friend. You help me believe in myself when I'm feeling down, and you always know how to make me laugh. You're smart, brave, and so much more than a science grade. I'm lucky to have you as my best friend.

The next day, she slipped the note into Ebony's locker. By lunchtime, Ebony found her in the cafeteria, holding the note with teary eyes.

"This is the nicest thing anyone's ever done for me," Ebony said. "Thank you, Nora. I really needed this."

Encouraged by Ebony's smile, Nora decided to keep the gratitude train going. That evening, she baked a batch of cookies, decorating each one with cheerful faces. The next morning, she handed them out to classmates, including their science teacher, Mr. Patel.

"Thank you, Mr. Patel," Nora said as she placed a cookie on his desk. "For always encouraging us and making science fun, even when it's hard."

Mr. Patel's face lit up. "That means a lot, Nora. Thank you."

Nora realized how simple acts of gratitude could brighten someone's day. It felt good to spread kindness.

That weekend, Nora invited Ebony and a few friends for a "Gratitude Party." She set up a circle of cushions in her living room and handed everyone a piece of paper and a marker.

"Let's do a gratitude circle," Nora said. "We'll each share one thing we're thankful for and write it down. Then we'll stick them on the wall."

Ebony hesitated. "I don't know if I can think of anything."

Nora smiled. "Start small. It can be anything—like the cookies we're about to eat or the fact that we're all here together."

Ebony thought for a moment and then wrote, *"I'm grateful for friends who remind me I'm more than my mistakes."*

By the end of the night, the wall was covered in colorful notes: *Warm blankets, my dog's wagging tail, Mom's hugs,* and *laughing until my stomach hurt.* The room felt lighter, filled with smiles and laughter.

What Nora Learned

Nora learned that gratitude is a powerful way to lift others up and strengthen relationships. By expressing her appreciation through thank-you notes, small gestures, and group activities, she helped Ebony see her worth beyond a single test score. Nora also discovered that spreading gratitude made her feel happier and more connected to the people around her.

Affirmation for Gratitude

Write this affirmation in your diary and repeat it in your mind as you reflect on your relationships:

"I am grateful for the people in my life, and I will share my appreciation with them every chance I get."

Try This

1. Create a small token of appreciation for someone who has made a difference in your life and share it with them, like a drawing, poem, or craft.

2. Do something meaningful for a friend or family member, like helping them with a task they've been struggling with or spending quality time together to show you care.
3. Gather your family or friends and share one thing you are thankful for about each person. Write them down and display them in a visible place.

Nora's story reminds us that gratitude is a gift we can give and receive every day. Who will you share your gratitude with today?

Part 8: Celebrating Your Inner Superstar

Hi there, Heroine-in-the-Making!

Do you know who the absolute superstar of your story is? It's YOU!

Inside of you, there's a brave, strong, and amazing heroine just waiting to shine. Sometimes, it's easy to forget that, but this last part of the book is all about celebrating how incredible you truly are.

Are you ready to celebrate your inner heroine? Let's go!

Chapter 19: Violet and the Puppy Rescue Mission

Violet peered through the curtains at her neighbor's backyard. The new puppy, Oscar, barked playfully as he bounced after a ball. His floppy ears flapped with every jump, and his tiny tail wagged furiously. Violet loved animals, but she'd always been a little afraid of dogs. Their loud barks and sudden movements made her freeze up.

"What's Oscar up to today?" Violet's mom asked, noticing her watching from the window.

"Just being his usual, energetic self," Violet replied. "I wish I wasn't so scared of him. He's so cute, but… I just can't."

Her mom smiled. "You're stronger than you think, Violet. Maybe one day you'll surprise yourself."

Violet wasn't so sure. She decided it was safer to admire Oscar from a distance.

The next morning, Violet heard a frantic knock at the door. It was her neighbor, Mrs. Hudson, looking worried. "Violet, Oscar got out of the yard, and I can't find him! Can you help me look?"

Violet hesitated. The idea of running into Oscar—barking, jumping Oscar—made her stomach churn. But Mrs. Hudson looked so upset, and Oscar was just a puppy. He might be scared, too.

"Okay," Violet said, taking a deep breath. "I'll help."

Armed with a leash and a bag of treats, Violet, her Mom, and Mrs. Hudson started their search. As they walked through the neighborhood, Violet tried to focus on her strengths. "I'm good at noticing small details," she thought. "Maybe I'll spot him."

Violet scanned every yard, bush, and driveway. Finally, she noticed tiny paw prints in the dirt near the park. "Over here!" she called to Mrs. Hudson.

They followed the tracks and soon heard faint barking. Oscar was stuck behind a fence, his leash tangled around a post. When he saw them, he whined and wagged his tail.

"There you are, Oscar!" Mrs. Hudson exclaimed, relieved.

Violet's heart raced as she approached the fence. Oscar's barking grew louder, and she froze for a moment. Then she remembered her mom's words: *You're stronger than you think.*

Violet knelt and spoke softly. "It's okay, Oscar. We're here to help." She reached out slowly, untangled the leash, and scooped him up. Oscar licked her hand, and Violet felt a little less afraid for the first time.

When they returned Oscar safely to his yard, Mrs. Hudson hugged Violet. "You were amazing! I don't know what I would've done without you."

Violet blushed. "I just... did what needed to be done."

That evening, Violet reflected on the day. She had faced her fear and helped someone in need. In her journal, she wrote: *Today, I found Oscar and overcame my fear of dogs. I'm proud of myself.*

Her mom noticed her writing and asked, "What's your proudest moment today?" "Helping Oscar," Violet said with a smile. "And maybe making a new furry friend."

Over the next week, Violet visited Oscar more often. She still flinched a little when he barked, but she learned to laugh it off. "Nobody's perfect," she told him one afternoon as he tripped over his own paws. "Not even you, buddy."

Oscar wagged his tail as if agreeing. Violet realized that her imperfections—like her fear of dogs—made her journey even more meaningful. By facing her fears, she'd grown stronger and more confident.

What Violet Learned

Violet learned that true strength comes from recognizing and embracing what makes you unique. By focusing on her keen observation skills, she helped find Oscar and discovered courage she didn't know she had. She also realized that imperfections aren't weaknesses; they make us human and relatable.

Affirmation for Recognizing Strengths

Write this affirmation in your diary and repeat it in your mind as you face new challenges:

"I am strong, unique, and capable of overcoming any fear."

Try This

1. Reflect on a time you faced a fear or solved a problem. Write about how it made you feel.

2. Think of one thing you've seen as a weakness. How could it be a strength?
3. Use your strengths to help a friend, neighbor, or family member with a challenge.

Violet's story reminds us that courage comes in all shapes and sizes. What strength will you discover today?

Chapter 20: Hazel and the Courage to Shine

Hazel walked out of the school auditorium, clutching her crumpled script in her hands. The play's final rehearsal had been a disaster. She'd forgotten her lines, stumbled over her words, and even knocked over a prop tree. As the laughter of her classmates echoed in her ears, she couldn't shake the embarrassment.

"I can't do this," she whispered to herself, sitting on the edge of the playground. "Everyone must think I'm hopeless."

Her best friend, Molly, found her a few minutes later. "Hazel, it's not as bad as you think," she said, sitting beside her. "Everyone makes mistakes. That's how we get better."

But Hazel shook her head. "I messed up so badly. Maybe I shouldn't even be in the play."

That evening, Hazel sat at her desk, staring at her mirror. Her grandmother knocked on the door with a cup of cocoa. "You seem upset, honey. What's going on?"

Hazel sighed. "I completely ruined rehearsal today. Maybe acting isn't for me."

Her grandmother smiled gently. "Hazel, do you remember when you first started drawing?"

Hazel nodded. "I used to get frustrated when my drawings didn't look right."

"Exactly. But you kept practicing, and now your art is amazing. The same goes for acting. You're allowed to stumble—it's part of learning. Don't dim your light just because you made a mistake. Let it shine brighter."

Hazel thought about her grandmother's words. Maybe she could give herself another chance.

The next day, Hazel arrived early at school. She found an empty classroom and set up her script on the teacher's desk. Taking a deep breath, she started practicing her lines. At first, her voice wavered, but as she repeated the scenes, her confidence grew.

Molly peeked through the door. "Hey, can I help?" she asked.

"Sure," Hazel said with a smile.

Together, they rehearsed until Hazel felt more comfortable. By lunchtime, she could deliver her lines without hesitation. She even added a few dramatic gestures that made Molly laugh.

"See?" Molly said. "You've got this."

Later that night, Hazel wrote in her journal:

I messed up yesterday, but I took a step towards improvement today. My story isn't about giving up but about learning and growing.

On the day of the play, Hazel's stomach churned with nerves. She peeked out from behind the curtain and saw the packed auditorium. Her parents waved from the front row, and Molly gave her a thumbs-up from the wings.

When it was her turn to step on stage, Hazel took a deep breath and confidently delivered her lines. When the scene ended, the audience laughed and clapped. Hazel felt a surge of pride as she took her bow.

After the play, several classmates came up to her. "You were amazing," one said. "How did you bounce back after that day?"

Hazel smiled. "I just kept practicing and reminded myself that one mistake doesn't define me."

Her courage inspired her classmates, and a few even shared stories of their own struggles. Hazel realized she'd encouraged others to do the same by shining her light.

What Hazel Learned

Hazel learned that failure is just a stepping stone to success. She discovered her inner strength by embracing her mistakes and working to improve. She also realized that her courage to keep going could inspire others to overcome their challenges. Most importantly, she learned that her story was hers to shape, and she made it one of resilience and growth.

Affirmation for Courage and Growth

Write this affirmation in your diary and repeat it in your mind as you face new challenges:

"I am brave, resilient, and capable of turning mistakes into opportunities to grow."

Try This

1. Write about a time you faced a challenge. What did you learn from it?

2. Identify three things you excel at, write them down in a diary, and continue to add to the list whenever you uncover something new about yourself.
3. Talk to a friend or family member about when you overcame a fear or failure. Encourage them to share their stories, too.

Hazel's story reminds us that even after a stumble, we have the power to rise, shine, and inspire others. What part of your story will you write next?

Chapter 21: Eleanor and the Call of the Music

Eleanor stared at the shiny, new flute in her hands. The silver instrument gleamed in the sunlight streaming through her bedroom window. She'd saved up for months to buy it, skipping trips to the mall and declining invites for ice cream with her friends. Now that it was finally hers, a wave of excitement washed over her. But with that excitement came a twinge of fear.

Her friends didn't understand her love for music. "Why do you waste so much time practicing?" her classmate Laura had once asked. "It's not like you're going to be famous."

Eleanor sighed. She didn't need fame—she just loved how playing music made her feel. But standing up to peer pressure wasn't easy.

Later that day, Eleanor's older brother, Caleb, knocked on her door. "Hey, you've been quiet," he said, stepping inside. "What's up?"

Eleanor hesitated. "Do you think it's weird that I spend so much time on music?"

Caleb frowned. "Weird? Not at all. It's what you love, right?" She nodded. "But Laura and the others think it's a waste of time. Sometimes, I feel like I should just stop."

Caleb leaned against the doorframe. "Eleanor, being true to yourself is one of the most important things you can do. It's what makes you, you. Don't let other people's opinions dim your light."

Eleanor thought about his words. Music had always been her passion. Giving it up just to fit in didn't feel right.

The next morning, Eleanor woke up with renewed determination. She practiced her flute with more focus than ever, perfecting a song she'd been working on for weeks. As the notes filled her room, a sense of confidence blossomed inside her.

Her music teacher, Ms. Reed, approached her at school during lunch. "Eleanor, I've noticed how hard you've been working. Would you be interested in performing at the spring concert?"

Eleanor's eyes widened. "Me? Perform in front of everyone?"

Ms. Reed smiled. "Yes. You have a gift, and it's worth sharing."

Eleanor hesitated but nodded. "I'll do it."

In the weeks that followed, Eleanor dedicated herself wholeheartedly to practicing for the concert. There were moments of uncertainty, particularly when Laura teased her about being a "band nerd." However, she reminded herself of Caleb's words: *"Don't let others' opinions dim your light."*

The night before the concert, Eleanor sat at her desk with a notebook. Ms. Reed had given the class an assignment to write about their values. Eleanor wrote:

1. **Passion:** I love music, and it brings me joy.
2. **Kindness:** I want to treat others respectfully, even when they don't understand me.
3. **Courage:** I want to be brave enough to follow my dreams.

Looking at her list, Eleanor felt a surge of pride. These values were hers, and they made her unique.

When the day of the concert arrived, Eleanor's heart pounded as she walked onto the stage. The audience's chatter quieted, and the spotlight illuminated her. She took a deep breath and began to play.

The melody filled the room, soaring and dipping like a bird in flight. As she played, Eleanor forgot about her nerves. She wasn't performing for Laura or anyone else—she was playing for herself. As the final note soared through the air, the audience exploded into thunderous applause.

After the concert, Ms. Reed hugged her. "You were incredible, Eleanor. You should be proud."

Even Laura approached her. "That was really good," she said, looking sheepish. "I didn't know you could play like that."

Eleanor smiled. "Thanks, Laura." For the first time, she realized that being true to herself could inspire others.

What Eleanor Learned

Eleanor learned that authenticity involves embracing who you are and living in a manner that feels right for you. By remaining true to her love for music, she gained confidence and self-respect. She also realized that being genuine could inspire others to value their unique strengths.

Affirmation for Living Authentically

Write this affirmation in your diary and repeat it in your mind as you follow your passions:

"I am true to myself, and I shine brightest when I embrace who I am."

Try This

1. Write down three activities or hobbies that make you happiest. How can you spend more time doing them?
2. Make a list of three values that are most important to you. Think about how you can live by them each day.
3. Think of a situation where you've felt pressure to fit in. What can you do to stay true to yourself?

Eleanor's story reminds us that living authentically is the key to unlocking our true potential. How will you embrace your authenticity today?

The Journey Ahead

Hi there, Amazing Adventurer!

Congratulations on completing this incredible journey! Look how far you've come. Along the way, you've unlocked tools to empower yourself and inspire others. This is just the beginning of your remarkable adventure.

Always remember what you've discovered along the way:

1. **Courage** is the foundation for overcoming fear and taking bold steps.
2. **Confidence** comes from within and grows with practice and self-belief.
3. **Resilience** helps you bounce back stronger from setbacks.
4. **Compassion and connection** create meaningful relationships and inspire positive change.
5. **Gratitude** transforms your mindset and builds happiness.
6. **Dreaming big and acting boldly** turns your vision into reality.
7. **Authenticity** is your superpower—embrace your true self.

Now, it's your turn to take everything you've learned and put it into action. You've got the heart to achieve anything you dream of. So, my dear amazing girl, the journey ahead is yours to shape. Go out there and shine like the star you are. And always remember: you've got this!

With love and belief in you…

Your Biggest Cheerleader

Sati

Thank You

Hey there, Amazing Girl!

Wow, you made it to the end of the book—high five! I'm so proud of you for going on this journey with me. I hope you had fun, learned new things, and feel ready to conquer the world!

Thank you so much for reading this book and sharing this journey with me. Now, I need your help. Could you ask your grown-up to leave a review for this book? It's super easy and helps me write more stories like this for you and other amazing girls. Just give them a nudge (like, "Please!") and let them know how much you loved it.

Scan Me

>> Leave a Review on Amazon<<

Thank you for being so awesome—you're my best heroine!

About the Author

Sati Siroda is an inspirational author passionate about empowering young minds through storytelling. With a knack for weaving simple yet profound tales, Sati inspires kids, teens, and young adults to embrace their unique potential and navigate life with courage and purpose.

Sati's diverse academic journey—from engineering to education, business, and communication—combined with her extensive travels and time spent in various countries for education, business, and skill development shapes her holistic storytelling approach. Her experience teaching in schools and universities has further enriched her understanding of young minds, helping her find her path as a storyteller who connects deeply with her audience. Her multifaceted background enables her to connect with readers in relatable and innovative ways. Her stories are fueled by a belief in the transformative power of narrative. Drawing from her expertise in strategic communication and her love for literature, Sati crafts engaging, uplifting books that instill resilience, emotional intelligence, and self-confidence in her readers. Her mission is clear: to inspire the next generation to dream fearlessly, think critically, and approach life's challenges with creativity and optimism.

Through her heartfelt stories, Sati creates a world where every page becomes a stepping stone toward growth, and every character serves as a guiding light. She warmly invites readers of all ages to embark on a journey of self-love, self-discovery, and empowerment through the enchantment of her books.

Stay connected with Sati Siroda on Instagram: *@SatiSiroda.*

Manufactured by Amazon.ca
Acheson, AB